Be Good to Yourself

Lucy Brown

Published by Lucy Brown, 2022.

BE GOOD TO YOURSELF

First edition. April 16, 2022.

Copyright © 2022 Lucy Brown.

ISBN: 979-8201502614

Written by Lucy Brown.

Table of Contents

Be Good to Yourself

A Beginner's Guide About How to Love Myself, Increase Motivation & Boost Mental Health

LUCY BROWN

Disclaimer

The content of this book has been checked and compiled with great care. For the completeness, correctness and topicality of the contents however no guarantee or guarantee can be taken over. The content of this book represents the personal experience and opinion of the author and is for entertainment purposes only. The content should not be confused with medical help.

There will be no legal responsibility or liability for damages resulting from counterproductive exercise or errors by the reader. No guarantee can be given for success. The author therefore assumes no responsibility for the non-achievement of the goals described in the book.

The Aim & Objectives of
Book

Be Good to Yourself is a beginner's guide to love and mental health. The aim and objectives of this book are to teach you how to love yourself, increase your motivation, and boost your mental health. The book talks about the critical role that self-love can have in your life. It also explores the many ways in which you can love yourself and the many ways that you can overcome mental health problems. You lack motivation and are unable to urge yourself to achieve what is really important to you in life. The thought that you deserve to be happy is ingrained in your subconscious mind, but for some reason, you just can't bring yourself to be happy.

Positive and negative thoughts engulf you, and you are constantly reminded that your glass is only half-full. Then this book is for you. Continue reading if this describes your emotions. You must take care of your physical and mental health in order to be happy and feel good about yourself. As a result, the mind and body may quickly go out of sync, resulting in a range of problems and hurdles. You may also learn that your illness prevents you from being the person you were born to be. Continue reading this book if you struggle with self-care because you will understand why now is the best time to make a change and how it may help you on your path of self-discovery in the process.

Who Should Read This Book?

Thuis book is for:

- Anyone who wants to transform their negative thoughts into positive, healing energy is welcome!
- Anyone who wants to develop a positive outlook, boost their self-esteem, and grow their confidence?
- This program may help those who have suffered from low self-esteem rebuild their self-worth and feel more at peace in their own skin.
- You may use this guide if you believe you're creative but lack self-esteem and are looking to boost your confidence in your abilities.

INTRODUCTION

Love yourself first and everything else falls into line. You really have to love yourself to get anything done in this world. LUCILLE BALL

It is crucial for everyone to have feelings of self-acceptance and love. The same amount of respect and love that you demonstrate toward yourself is unlikely to be reciprocated by others. There's no doubt that we have certain deficiencies as well as some flaws. Learn to accept yourself for who you are and to respect yourself as a consequence of going through this process. The concepts of self-esteem and self-love are intricately intertwined. It is hard to really love oneself if one does not have self-confidence. When it comes to loving yourself, you will have a difficult time doing so at first since you do not place a high value on yourself. However, if you accept and respect yourself, your self-esteem as well as your self-confidence will increase as a result of this. The first step to realizing your self-worth is to make a deliberate choice to appreciate yourself. If you want to live a happy and fulfilled life, you must first make a choice. In order to achieve your maximum potential, you must first have a positive self-image. It is, therefore, a very important "job" to learn to love oneself. Understanding yourself and the factors that influence your conduct is the first step in developing your personality. Regardless of how many defects you have, you must learn to deal with them and continue on your journey. You must accept the fact that no one is flawless, and this is something you should be aware of. Even the loveliest individuals we've ever met or loved have their own unique set of imperfections.

These aren't the only ideas that have crossed your mind. First, consider yourself from a distance, and then look yourself directly in the eyes. Face your reflection and let yourself be taken in by the beauty that you reflect back. Despite the fact that you are not well-known to others, you are the center of your own universe, and everything in your life revolves around you. Do you allow yourself to get deflated by what seem to be little details? Does there ever seem to be a voice in your brain that tells you that you're worthless and foolish when you make a mistake? Do you think this individual is speaking the truth, or do you have your doubts? If you find yourself condemning yourself on a regular basis, stop doing so. Focusing on your strengths rather than your flaws or deficiencies is critical when assessing your own abilities and capabilities. Having a more positive attitude towards life may assist you in developing a more positive connection with yourself as well as a larger sense of self-importance. As a consequence, people's self-esteem and confidence are strengthened. Furthermore, showing kindness to others is a positive trait.

To be happy, you must first learn to accept and love yourself. If you have a general hatred for people, you will develop a bitter personality, and your love for yourself will diminish as a result. Make an effort to assist people who are important to you. Ultimately, you will feel better about yourself and will be able to love yourself with more ease as a result of this process. At the very least, you made an effort. People all throughout the globe go through their lives doing little more than the absolute minimum to survive. Even if your greatest efforts to achieve a goal were met with failure for any reason, don't allow this to deter you from continuing your efforts. Making even the smallest effort is a significant accomplishment.

When it comes to competition, winning isn't necessarily the most important thing. One's own fears may deal one of the most devastating blows to one's sense of self-worth. Individuals may be reluctant to attempt new things for fear that if they do, it will be seen as a personal failure on their part. Take a deep breath and put your worries aside. It is possible that you will succeed, but your anxieties will prevent you from doing so. If you want to be successful in your life, you must put your fears aside and put in a real effort. Almost everyone makes a mistake at some point in their life. Your speech was also littered with grammatical errors. Continued self-pity and self-loathing are harmful habits that you must quit if you want to live a happy life. It is inevitable that everyone will make mistakes at some point in their lives. Forgiving oneself is a crucial life skill to develop. Failure to forgive oneself will hinder one's attempts to move on and achieve success in the future, as it did in the past. Anything that has happened has not been done on purpose, and you must have faith in your own capacity to cope with whatever has happened. Keep telling yourself that you've learnt from your error and that you won't make the same mistake in the future.

It is possible to remain optimistic in this life even if you do not believe in a higher power. This is true even if you consider yourself an atheist. Religious belief is completely optional, and you are under no obligation to follow a particular faith. By putting your trust in the universe to take care of everything for you, you may let go of your concerns and concerns.

Chapter 1: How to Love Yourself and the Reasons for Doing So

Y ou are able to consistently, if not always, end up in love with people and with the planet's non-human creatures because of your true adoration for them and for yourself. Because we are all related on every level, both material and divine, it is impossible for us to exist in isolation. For many individuals, the notions of self-love and neighbor-love are incompatible when used together in the same sentence. Self-love is not synonymous with narcissism, and those who think this are completely deluded. Keep the following points in mind, however: First and foremost, in order to really love someone else, you must learn to love yourself first and foremost. It is only when you become more self-aware that your capacity to love me will increase. That which comes from your center is a source of energy that gives nourishment to everything near you, including yourself.

One of the most effective ways to show your appreciation is to devote your time and energy to activities that you find enjoyable. Irrespective of your financial status, the most valuable gifts you can give to the world are those that result from your living life to the fullest and following your interests. What do you have planned for the rest of the year? So, deep down, what type of woman or man do you wish to be in your heart of hearts? What is it that ignites a flame in your heart? Whatever your thoughts and feelings are, remember to utilize them as a source of inspiration for the work you do in your own neighborhoods. You should revisit these questions periodically since your replies will change over time.

Explore your interests and dislikes as well as your dreams and desires, as well as your motivations for pursuing certain goals and objectives. Writing, meditating, taking a stroll in the woods, praying, or just being silent might help you become still and listen to your inner voice. Make the decision to be completely honest with yourself. Certain aspects of your personality will be easy to fall in love with, especially if they are unique. On the other hand, there are some who aren't convinced. Even while you're hiding in the shadows, you maintain command. If you take the time and effort to get to know them, you will discover that they have a great deal to give.

To have a passionate relationship with oneself This is a well-deserved prize for your efforts. Make a list of all of the positive characteristics and good deeds that you possess and keep it handy. If you're anything like me, you're really skilled at making yourself feel bad about your failings in the love department. Instead of concentrating on your defects and failures right now, imagine yourself as a little girl or boy from your childhood. Take a look at the small one who is sitting on your lap. Tell her that she is a loser and that she is unworthy of your attention since she is a failure. No way! Your first response would be to wrap your arms around her and tell her how beautiful she is, no matter how many errors she makes. This would be your second reaction. You now have a child growing inside of you. Everything about him or her is the same as yours. Treat your present-day self with the same compassion and love that you showed your previous-day self.

Be head over heels in love with yourself. When you're alone, there are a variety of activities to keep you entertained. You may sit in front of the television or go to the movies by yourself. You may sketch, sing, laugh, weep, run, sit quietly, sleep, or jump rope to pass the time, among other things. Make a note of how you're feeling, both physically and psychologically, and pay attention to it. Journal about your feelings and write love letters to yourself in journals or other kinds of self-expression. In your mind, tell yourself that you are a wonderful person and that there is no one else you would want to have in your position.

1.1 You must learn to love and accept yourself

It's possible that you were raised with the belief that putting one's own needs before others is selfish from a young age. Do you believe it is selfish to prioritize one's own interests above those of others? That's just not true, and it's critical that you let go of this self-hating notion before you can learn to accept and respect your own uniqueness. No matter what else is going on in your life, it will not matter if you do not love yourself enough to prioritize yourself first. You are demonstrating a lack of self-love to your children, and you are placing yourself under a great deal of stress, which is not good for your health or for your relationships with other people. Given that a lack of self-love implies that you aren't addressing your own needs, you may find yourself feeling depressed, nervous, or even angry on a regular basis. Depression, anxiety, and fury are all common feelings associated with being cheated on or rejected by someone you care about. As a result of your losses, you will be depressed and anxious.

You'll be terrified because you're endangering your own health by failing to satisfy your own expectations. There are no questions in your mind about the fact that your life is missing the love and success that you really want. My belief is that you should learn to really love and accept yourself first, and that you should do so as soon as possible. Look yourself in the eyes every morning and tell yourself, "I adore you." Relax and enjoy yourself as much as you possibly can, if that is even feasible at this point in your life. List all of the enjoyable experiences you've had in the past, and then record them in a notebook or diary. Investing in a diary today will enable you to begin tracking your own development as soon as possible in the future. Fill in the blanks on the left-hand side of a certain page in your diary with any negative thoughts you have about yourself that you wish to change or eliminate. must be employed in this specific manner. Fill in the blanks with positive beliefs on the right-hand side of your paper, then repeat them many times during the day to help them stick in your memory.

Affirmations should be written on the same mirror that you use to remind yourself how much you appreciate and love yourself each morning. This is a nice suggestion. This method will help you become acutely aware of whatever is preventing you from learning to love yourself first and will also assist you in validating your own self-worth. What or who, in your opinion, is preventing you from becoming your best self-right now? After all, we're all here to have a good time. How did you come to realize that you didn't have to love yourself first before you could love others, as some people believe? The truth is that when you don't love yourself first, you will conceal your true self from others because you will be unsure of who you are or what you want out of life. How can you learn about yourself if your attention is constantly drawn away from yourself? In order to go ahead, you must heal your previous wounds and learn to love yourself first and foremost, regardless of your circumstances.

1.2 It's a good idea to start with self-acceptance as a starting point

The ability to express gratitude to oneself is a critical component of self-acceptance. You may develop a more optimistic attitude towards your life and the world around you if you accept your imperfections and acknowledge them. You're more prone to overlooking people who make disparaging comments about your character. If you are confident in your own skin, you will be able to enjoy your life to the maximum extent. As an alternative to holding animosity, replace it with love, not just toward others, but also toward oneself. Take a minute to pamper yourself with a little self-care time. Spend some time pampering yourself by going to a salon and taking advantage of the services offered by the stylists. The fact that you have a positive view on life is already evidence that you are attractive on the inside. So, what are you waiting for? Get started now! If you want to stand out from the crowd, start doing something about it right now!

Having pink-colored nails is perfectly OK if you're a male, but you shouldn't go to the manicure salon right now since you'll look ridiculous. Is it possible that you were contemplating getting a haircut at your favorite barbershop? You may wish to have a soothing massage after you've had an aromatherapy treatment to help you unwind. In order to be self-loving, you do not have to put your own desires ahead of those of other people. It simply means that you should schedule some time for yourself on a regular basis for personal renewal. Taking a deep breath and relishing the air may be something you haven't done in quite some time.

You come to the realization that it is past time for you to take a minute to appreciate the beauty of nature. The way you view yourself has an impact on how others perceive you. The fact that you treat yourself poorly may lead to the expectation that other people will treat you similarly. It is necessary to accept and love yourself first before you can expect people to embrace and love you for who you actually are. It is necessary to express some self-forgiveness. There is no such thing as a flawless person, and everyone makes errors that are distinct from their own. Many people will look at you with a raised eyebrow if they meet you for the first time because you've made your fair share of awkward and embarrassing mistakes. Although this may be the case, accepting responsibility is essential. Isn't it? If you have any skeletons in your closet that you are attempting to keep hidden from yourself, it is hard to fully accept yourself. If you want to attain your goals, you must be honest with yourself and forget about your errors.

You must think that you are deserving of love before you can receive it. To believe that you are completely undeserving of receiving this good benefit and pleasure demonstrates a lack of regard and appreciation for yourself and others. To paraphrase a well-known proverb, you can't give away something that you don't really have. Because if you don't love yourself, or if you can't bring yourself to do so, your professions of love for others will be far less credible. It's also likely that they'll be reluctant to demonstrate their own unique kind of love for you in the same manner that you are.

Another method of assisting yourself in learning to love yourself is to refrain from doing anything that is damaging to you or the people around you. If you're having trouble letting go of your vices, we recommend that you do so immediately. The reason for this is that if you really care about your health and well-being, you would refrain from participating in activities that are harmful to your health and well-being. Always remember that the more self-loving you are, the more likely it is that others will feel the same way about themselves.

1.3 Respect Yourself

One of the most important lessons I've learned in my life is that feeling good about oneself is key to one's happiness and mental well-being. Many individuals are unaware that loving themselves is a powerful force that may be used to alleviate a broad variety of emotional and physical difficulties, including depression. A new sense of purpose and determination come over us after our trip. We want to keep growing ourselves and becoming better at everything we do.

Self-love should not be confused with narcissism, which is defined as being preoccupied with oneself and one's own concerns or concerns about one's own affairs. It is not necessary to prevent coming off as egotistical or conceited-sounding. There is a significant distinction between the two of them. The feeling of connection to the magnificent person who lives inside you will grow as a consequence of learning to appreciate yourself. We are all composed of light, but unless you ignite that light and give it life, it will remain dim and dead until you do. This implies that you must first fall in love with the item before you can begin the process of falling in love with yourself. At times, it might be difficult to discern when you're not in love with who you really are.

We all take it for granted that we do, as if it were a given. What causes so many individuals to allow themselves to be robbed of their power and, as a result, take their own lives? Allow yourself to ponder the truth that when you don't have enough self-love or self-confidence, you are effectively saying, "I don't care what happens." You should be aware of the following warning signs that you should learn to respect yourself a little bit better: As long as you continue to tolerate violence and hostility in an abusive relationship, you will be seen as involved in the violence and hostility. You believe you're doing a good thing by defending your family, but in truth, you're acting out of sheer terror.

Your ability to see clearly is hampered by a lack of self-acceptance that prevents you from seeing properly. It is when you try to solve your issues on your own by abusing drugs or alcohol that you are at risk. Self-abuse is something that will happen to you if you don't love yourself enough to protect yourself from it. Recognize that the devastation of one's own life is caused by a lack of self-love on the part of the individual. If you are nearing the end of your life and believe you deserve to die, you may want to consider planning a suicide. Suicide, in the eyes of people who comprehend karma, is clearly against the fundamental rules of the universe. Your current situation does not allow you to do what you want at this moment. Before one can receive answers, one must first learn to accept and respect oneself.

When you've gained weight and become unattractive, and you're no longer content with your look or your self-esteem, you've reached a breaking point. If you are really concerned about your appearance and well-being, these considerations will be of the most significance to you. A healthy dose of self-love and respect will assist you in better appreciating your physical body and your overall health. Believe in the sanctity of your soul and treat it with reverence. When you learn to love yourself and put yourself first, you'll be better equipped to make the best choices for yourself and others around you, including your children. In addition, you'll learn how to be in charge of your own life, as well as how to clear your mind and emotions through meditation and other practices.

When it comes to finding someone who is more worthy of your love and commitment than you are, it doesn't matter where you look on the globe. A quotation by an unidentified author You are not a bad person because you do not care about other people, do not accept responsibility, do not make sacrifices for others, or do not care about yourself. Nothing has changed in terms of your responsibility to other people. The first step in learning how to really appreciate and love people is to change your attitude toward yourself and take responsibility for your actions and reactions. If you enjoy breeding, your efforts will be rewarded in the future. It should become a habit to remind yourself on a regular basis how much you appreciate what you are doing.

1.4 Understanding yourself

"Love yourself first before you can love anybody else" is a phrase that has been repeated to us at some point in our lives. To be honest, I was a little taken aback by the concept at first. I was really perplexed by everything. To begin with, I was perplexed as to "Is there anybody else that does this? And why is this the case?" After fully comprehending the notion, I can firmly assert that loving oneself is the first step toward living a meaningful life. Loving oneself is a fundamental need, not a habit or a virtue, in the same way that breathing and eating are. We come to this planet and are then left to fend for ourselves, which is a terrible feeling.

I'm the only one who is accompanying me on this voyage; it's just me and my ideas. Because of this, there is a paradox in that this inner buddy cannot be disregarded at any cost. Learning about and understanding oneself is critical in every connection, but especially in romantic ones, if one aspires to discover love for someone else. Consider devoting some time to getting to know your inner self, discovering what it appreciates and dislikes, what it is good at and what it is awful at, and what values it embodies. You must first acknowledge and embrace all of your internal sensations, and then you must acknowledge and love your uniqueness as a result of these experiences. Learning to accept and love oneself takes time and effort.

For people who are persuaded of the need to love themselves but are unsure of how to go about doing so, the following are some fundamental guidelines: Even though self-forgiveness is a crucial skill that you've learned, you've been much too harsh on yourself when it comes to letting go and forgiving other people. Avoid making snap decisions on what went wrong, and instead concentrate on recognizing and addressing the issue at hand. It is your responsibility to submit the information. In this life, you cannot expect to learn the values you seek from anybody or anything other than yourself, and it is time to accept this truth. Accept the reality of the situation. Before you can achieve this state of mind, you must first and foremost love, support, and nurture yourself. When you taste it, you'll be blown away by the depth of flavor it provides. The importance of words cannot be overstated in the case that you are unable to hear yourself communicate what you are trying to say. Daily communication with oneself about your self-esteem is essential.

In your essay, you should offer a full account of the characteristics you value in yourself and why you find them attractive. Even though it's an effective approach, if you don't want to utilize it, maintain a notebook in which you may scribble down the things that are making you anxious. As a consequence of this, you will have a more positive perception of yourself. Decision-making should be based on one's actual wishes— We tell people all the time that they should "listen to their hearts." There's nothing going on here except for your own thoughts and emotions, of course. One more manner in which this voice often communicates is by repeatedly imposing an idea in front of you. Because of this, it serves as an ongoing reminder to make the conscious decision to be comfortable in your own skin. It gives you a great degree of self-assurance to pay heed to your own thoughts. Your heart is filled with an overwhelming sense of self-assurance and tenderness.

Chapter 2: Creating a Positive Atmosphere for Yourself

Is it feasible to achieve success in life by maintaining a cheerful attitude? Long-term success in life, whether you're attempting to maintain sobriety or prevent domestic violence, is dependent on your ability to surround yourself with people who have good thoughts about you. The people with whom you choose to surround yourself have a big influence on your capacity to think positively at all times. There is no need to confine your social circle to people who are "perfect." Contrary to this, it recommends spending as much time as possible with joyful people who inspire you to be your best self and who put a strong focus on positivity. I appreciate that they are encouraging you in your attempts to maintain your sobriety. During your conversation regarding previous experiences with domestic abuse or other problems, your friends and family members will provide emotional support to help you through the process. It is possible for positive individuals to be unhappy at times, but this does not rule out the possibility that they are striving to be a good influence in your life. It makes no difference whether the individuals in question are close friends or colleagues. In reality, they really care about your well-being and are enthusiastic about seeing you achieve your objectives. When you surround yourself with positive influences, it makes it much simpler to remain focused on your long-term objectives. As a result, you'll have a more positive attitude towards yourself. Spending time with these individuals will leave you feeling invigorated and driven. You will not experience the same amount of anxiety as you had earlier. By surrounding oneself with people who have a positive self-image, it becomes much simpler to maintain focus on your long-term goals and objectives. As a result, you'll have a more positive attitude towards yourself. Spending time with these individuals will leave you feeling invigorated and driven. You will not experience the same amount of anxiety as you had earlier.

2.1 When you surround yourself with positive people?

I t is infectious to be in good health and happy. When you go into a room full of individuals who are enthusiastic and effervescent, you immediately feel better about your situation. Despite the fact that I wasn't feeling well at the time, I'm certain that I've done it many times in the past. More to the point, have you ever been in the company of a bunch of individuals that are melancholy, gloomy, and fed up with life? You will be impacted by the emotions of individuals in your immediate vicinity, and you will be affected by the emotions of those in your immediate vicinity. If you are in the company of individuals who are cheerful, energetic, and driven, you will find it impossible to resist absorbing their energy! People who are happy, healthy, and optimistic about their lives are more successful than those who are not. Individuals' potential to accomplish is significantly enhanced when they are happy and optimistic. Being successful in business and in life requires more than just being a great employee or boss; it requires being a great leader as well. There is a widely held assumption that individuals who feel good about themselves, both physically and mentally, are more productive at their places of employment.

If you are suffering from despair, sickness, or weariness, there is nothing worse than continuing to suffer for the rest of the day since it will only make you feel worse. It's impossible to contain the amount of energy you have when you're feeling well. Imagine walking around with a spring in your step all year long. It is as a consequence of this that you will be both inspired and driven by them in turn. You should surround yourself with people you like being around, who inspire you, and who you can look at and think about. The reason these people are in your life is because they are "awesome," and that's why they're there. Being around others who inspire you, whether it's in a small group or a large organization, drives your desire to achieve and pushes you to be the greatest version of yourself imaginable. If you're always surrounded by individuals that make you want to roll your eyes, you'll never be able to progress or become more.

As a result, your ability to develop will be severely restricted. Rather than slacking off, take to the skies! Healthy acts are beneficial to one's soul. Take deliberate steps to surround yourself with good influences, such as people who support charity activities, follow the law, and treat others with dignity. As a result of your actions and surroundings, you will develop into a better person if you surround yourself with people who do good things, are nice to others, care about the environment, and care about other issues that you are passionate about. If you're surrounded by irresponsible individuals who flout the law, litter, and engage in other criminal activities, your way of life will be progressively undermined over time. It is essential to prevent this from happening. It is not necessary to stay the same in order to be good; rather, it is necessary to evolve into a better person. Those who are thankful are likely to be full of optimism. Please accept my heartfelt thanks for all you have done to help me over the years. Many well-known people have said that appreciation is the most important factor in achieving achievement. Consider all of the gifts you have in your life. Are you grateful to the individuals who have enriched your life? Then what about your family and friends? Take stock of your life's events and think about the opportunities that have been presented to you. There are many things to be thankful for, ranging from the smallest to the most major.

2.2 How to create a positive environment for yourself

Whatever our life objectives, we all want to be successful in some manner, whether it's at work or in our interpersonal relationships. You may wonder why so few individuals are really happy in all of these areas if so, few people are truly happy in all of them.

To get the solution, look no further than your own personal standards. According to Tony, the only thing that will have a long-term influence on you, your company, or your relationship is an increase in your degree of excellence. Spending time with people that pull you down with their negative energy is not recommended. You should surround yourself with those who will help you to rise above your circumstances by sharing their expertise and assisting you in learning from your failures. Improve your own and other people's lives by setting a higher standard. This concept, which is known as the "law of attraction," stretches all the way back to Confucius in the 6th century BC, when he wrote the following comment regarding being in the wrong environment despite being the smartest person there. The "law of attraction" is a term used to describe this concept.

Because it is true, you can utilize the concept that you are defined by the people you spend the majority of your time with to accomplish your goals in business and in life. Have you ever heard someone say to you, "You are who you associate with"? It's possible that, in the same way that your parents were worried about your involvement with the wrong crowd, you are afraid of your children being involved with the wrong crowd. The people in your life have a significant impact on your emotions and attitude towards the world, as well as on the sort of life you expect for yourself.

We believe that closeness is a positive factor in our children's lives, and we want to make the most of it for both their and our sakes. As a result, why not put it to good use for our own benefit? Being surrounded by good individuals in your life may have a great impact on your professional career, love relationships, and everything in between. Because of this, the more positive and cheerier your circumstances, the more probable it is that you will adopt strong attitudes and regard life as occurring for and rather than to you. It is beneficial to surround yourself with individuals who make you happy because you will reap the rewards. In contrast, if you surround yourself with people who make you feel bad, you will pay for it.

2.3 Identify and surround yourself with people who are wiser than you are

Prepare your subordinates to take over your responsibilities, "a smart manager told a group of supervisors at a meeting. This idea was particularly noteworthy in a difficult economic climate, when individuals are attempting to establish themselves as indispensable. He believes that you should constantly be thinking about your future job, and that this should lead to an investment in the leadership potential of your colleagues. When you have the brightest individuals in your life, you should surround yourself with people who are smarter than you are.

The great majority of businesses, however, do not function in this manner. The hierarchical structure of a corporation is commonly employed to retain highly qualified individuals in their current roles. Particularly in small businesses, this might mean death for highly educated employees who want to advance their careers but don't see a clear path to accomplishing their goals. Workers are terrified of people who have too many ideas, for fear of being demoted or losing their position within the organization, which is understandable. The inverse is also true: employing intelligent individuals is a good decision. Why? Innovative ideas that help others do not belong just to the founders of businesses; they belong to everyone. It is possible that you are a better manager than an innovator when it comes to productivity. In order to plan the future of your organization, you will need help from other people.

As soon as you come up with a good concept, your engineers can improve it, your marketing department can publicize it, and your administrative team can put it into action in conjunction with you, all at the same time. If your organization does not get new ideas, it may begin to grow stale. If your firm is staffed with bright, enthusiastic young individuals, it will be able to maintain its position at the top of the industry. It is possible that, as a leader, you lack the necessary experience to successfully develop your product in a technologically oriented organization, such as your own. Having a team of professionals in a range of sectors, such as information technology (IT), finance, systems, logistics, and administration, will be critical to the smooth functioning of your company (AL). This does not reflect adversely on your character in any way whatsoever. It is your responsibility, rather than being a jack of all trades who is always reinventing the wheel, to lead the team and convince them to collaborate for your mutual advantage.

If you are serious about growing your company, the proper individuals will challenge you. But you will adopt a management style that encourages workers to share their ideas without micromanaging them in the course of doing so. The introduction of intelligent new personnel may create rivalry, which may in turn motivate you and other employees to achieve higher levels of performance, regardless of your position within the company. There are occasions when a new individual's talents compliment those of other members of the group, even if the other members were unaware that they had such abilities before the new person was added. They may bring a new set of abilities to the table that will be very beneficial to the organization. If you're working with a limited budget, you may be concerned that employing the best and the brightest would be difficult for you. The creation of new methods of funding positions, as well as a change in organizational structure or goals, may be required in order to achieve this. Openness to learning from individuals who are brighter than you and a willingness to consider their recommendations may help you improve your own management skills as well as the overall capabilities of your organization.

Chapter 3: Mind and Body Purification

Purification of the mind, body, and spirit is a much more extensive process than just cleaning the house. Many individuals make the mistake of supposing the two terms to be synonymous. Our health and well-being depend on us taking time away from work and other duties in order to relax and cleanse our bodies and spirits of toxins, which is critical to our survival. A variety of therapeutic effects have been shown to be associated with spring cleaning activities. Consider what it might be like to have more mental, physical, and emotional space on your own. Having a high level of mental, bodily, and spiritual purity may be a freeing experience for the person who does it.

Everything from food to ideas to emotions is constantly being absorbed by our bodies and brains, resulting in a perpetual flow of both. In a world moving at 100 miles per hour, we may find ourselves rapidly overwhelmed. If you're feeling burned out or simply need a break from work or life in general, think about taking a brief vacation to focus on self-care and relaxation. You should make an attempt to set aside some time each day for personal reflection. Make a conscious effort to get rid of the memories from your past that are still bothering you throughout your cleaning session. To express yourself, begin a personal practice such as writing a letter (you do not have to mail it!) to yourself. Instead, you may want to invest in a lovely notebook that you can use to keep track of your thoughts and feelings on a consistent basis. It is impossible to ignore one's emotions. Learn from your errors and strive to be a better person in the future. If you're cleaning your house, an excellent notion is to concentrate on your eating habits as much as possible. Make sure you drink enough water in order to prevent becoming dehydrated.

Verify that you are receiving enough fluids by keeping track of your fluid consumption. Making ginger tea with lemon juice is a wonderful way to keep warm throughout the winter months. If you're a coffee drinker by habit, consider switching to green tea for your detox day as an alternative. By teaching you how to prepare alkaline vegetable broth, you may boost enzyme and cellular metabolism, as well as overall cleaning and detoxifying, among other benefits. Ayurvedic medicine often makes use of a dry brush, which has been shown to have soothing effects on the body. Using this strategy to increase your energy and vitality is a simple and cost-effective way to improve your overall health. A basic body brush is all that is required to complete the task. If you don't want to use the brush in the bath or shower, you may use it on dry skin instead of wet. After you've finished dry brushing, hydrate your skin with a moisturizer or body oil to keep it moisturized. Start at the top of your body and work your way down, taking care not to scrape too hard so that your skin does not get irritated in the process. According to alternative medicine, taking a contrast shower can help you get more blood flow and be more energetic.

In contrast, alternating between hot and cold water is used to help in the healing process in the case of cold-water therapy. Make a start by setting the temperature of the water in your shower to a level that you are comfortable with. According to the manufacturer, the goal should be for it to be warm but not too hot or scorching. In order to prevent getting burned, you must use prudence and common sense while working. Make a one-minute switch to cold water before switching back to hot water again. Before coming out of the water, check to see that the temperature is as low as you can tolerate. Although the cold water may be uncomfortable, it may also provide you with a rush of energy. It is advised that you repeat this cycle two to three times.

3.1 Spending time with people who deplete your energy is not a wise decision

Do you feel worse than you did before you spent time with a certain individual? No excuse should be given for maintaining a toxic person in your life if the connection is not beneficial to you or does not make you happy, regardless of whether the person is a member of your direct family or a childhood friend of yours. In light of their lack of boundaries, their unwanted stress or drama, or the negative impact they have on your other relationships, you should let them go in the following ways: Their thoughts and sentiments are interfering with your work in ways that you are not aware of.

3.2 People that make you feel good about yourself

When you get rid of the individuals who make you feel awful, you will have more time to spend with those who make you happy. Make a conscious effort to spend time with the people who matter to you, even if it's just for a short meal or a cup of coffee. Having a 15-minute conversation with a person you care about may help to relieve tension and improve your mood, allowing you to feel more whole and at peace.

3.3 You should take a walk every day to get some fresh air in your lungs

Take a trip into the vast outdoors to get away from the hustle and bustle of everyday life. Previous studies have shown that it may be fairly relaxing for both the mind and the spirit when it comes to the mind. In a study by Stanford University, researchers found that even a 90-minute nature walk or trip made participants happier and less likely to get depressed in the long run.

3.4 Do a thorough cleaning of your home

You haven't finished your spring cleaning yet, have you? It is never too late to make a positive change in one's life. Physical clutter on your desk and kitchen counter may not seem like a good idea while attempting to clear your mind, but it really helps a great deal in the process of doing so. Consequently, you will no longer be tired and stressed by your surroundings, and you will be in a more positive frame of mind after you finish cleaning your area.

3.5 Enroll in a Ceramics Class

As an alternative to scrolling through your phone's social media feeds, try your hand at pottery or other comparable crafts. People think that molding clay and getting their hands messy is a very therapeutic hobby that helps them to release tension while also producing something beautiful that they can proudly display in their homes as a reminder to strive for those calm, pleasant sentiments.

3.6 Examine your eating habits and determine what needs to be changed

If you don't take care of your body, you won't be able to adequately nourish your mind and spirit. If you have a diet that is mostly comprised of processed foods, make an effort to include more vibrant, healthier options in your weekly agenda. According to recent research, eating an apple or a banana for breakfast instead of anything sweet may help you maintain better physical and mental health over time.

3.7 Relax by soaking in a soothing bath

A body cleanse is not always about depriving yourself of the opportunity to completely relax and enjoy yourself. What better way to do this than by soaking in a tub of warm water? Natural alternatives, such as adding slices of fruit or some essential oils to warm water to totally renew your soul, rather than purchasing a bath bomb from the shop with a lengthy list of odd components, are preferable.

3.8 Make an effort to be a little more self-centered

Although it may seem that taking care of one's personal needs is selfish, this is not the case. Your whole day and every day of the week is devoted to ensuring the well-being of individuals in your immediate family and group of friends. However, how much time you are willing to devote to yourself is a different question. Putting your attention on your own needs and priorities rather than the desires and priorities of others will help you to cleanse your mind and spirit. Regardless of how "selfish" it seems to be, you should always prioritize your mental health above all else.

How to Begin Meditating Immediately: Concentrate on the Present Moment and Everything Else Will Fall into Place.

Breathing is essential for our survival; otherwise, we wouldn't be here to tell you about it. In our language, the term "pranayama" literally translates as "management of life force." In order for our brains to work properly, they, like all of our other organs and cells, need oxygen. Breathing exercises should be performed on a regular basis in order to alleviate stress and prevent sickness. The physical advantages of breathing exercises aren't the only ones that may be used to calm our bodies. Because the quicker our breaths are taken, the more nervous our minds get, we must learn to breathe slowly and deeply in order to maintain a peaceful and tranquil frame of mind. Breathing deeply and slowly helps us relax our minds, which in turn enables us to more completely explore our emotions. Meditation has the ability to purify the mind, the body, and the spirit all at the same time. Having the ability to sit alone and converse with people is a great delight for me. Concentrate on seeing meditation as a technique of cleansing your mind and creating space for you to listen with calm, focused attention and without being distracted by anything outside of yourself. No doubt you've heard of meditation and the myriad health advantages it may give to both the mind and the body. But what exactly is meditation?

For the most part, everyone who has attempted meditation has discovered that it raises awareness, calms the mind, and improves one's capacity to focus. Meditation is open to everyone, regardless of age. If you believe that it is solely for monks and mystics, you should reconsider your point of view on the subject. No specific equipment or training is required to learn how to meditate, and you do not even need to leave the comfort of your own home to do it. It makes no difference how you go about it, since the end goal of any meditation practice is the same: to empty the mind of all distracting and harmful ideas in order to allow it to rest quietly in the present moment.

After years of stored thoughts, ideas, and notions have been freed from the mind, a more calm and purposeful way of living may be obtained. When it is reduced to its most basic form, meditation is a method of cleaning the mind. Some meditators choose to cut off all external stimuli, including sights, sounds, and odors, in order to better concentrate their thoughts during their sessions. Given how used we have been to being surrounded by a steady assault of noise, the abrupt cessation of this barrage may be deafening. After some practice, you will start to see how it changes your thinking, even though it will take some time to get used to.

Many would-be meditators are put off by the physically demanding contemplative poses they see on television. To be quite honest, meditation does not include any of those challenging postures or positions. Choose a meditation posture that is most comfortable for you, depending on your own preferences and the time of day. Poses such as cross-legged, sitting, standing, reclining, and even walking are appropriate. Ideally, your hands should rest on your knees, palms facing up, and you should be sitting in a comfortable posture with your back completely straight. Close your eyes for a moment and take a long, deep breath in and out. Take deep breaths in and out via your nose, paying close attention to the movement of your lungs as you do so. It is totally natural and necessary for ideas to enter your mind and attempt to divert your focus away from your breathing. All you have to do now is return your focus to your breathing and pay close attention to each inhale and exhale. If you're new to meditation, starting with a small period of time and gradually increasing it as you grow used to it is an excellent method.

3.9 Stress may be relieved from both the body and the mind by doing these simple exercises

That we must eliminate stress-inducing substances from our brains is not based on rational reasoning. Did you know, on the other hand, that this operation may wind up being beneficial to us in the long run? Your body is contaminated with harmful chemicals, but you may be unaware of the countless benefits that may be gained by purifying both your mind and your body at the same time. When we are extremely dehydrated for a prolonged length of time, our bodies begin to accumulate toxins and waste, which may be harmful. It is possible that we may have difficulty getting rid of it if we do not take the necessary procedures to cleanse ourselves. It is a typical side consequence of not drinking enough water during the day to suffer from dehydration, which may lead to illness. If this occurs on a frequent basis, it is possible that chronic dehydration will develop in the body. Many individuals have become used to this state of affairs and do not pay attention to any warning signs of dehydration that may appear.

Chapter 4: What You Can Do Right Now to Attract Positive Energy

As we go about our everyday activities, we trade energy with the rest of the planet. There is a vibrating energy present in our minds, bodies, and souls that others may see and feel. These vibrations have an effect on our own personal energy levels.

Because of this, we have different reactions to different people. Some make us feel warm, calm, and joyful, while others make us feel frigid, worried, and blue. We carry that energy about with us, and it has an impact on everyone with whom we come into contact, not just ourselves and our surroundings. Positive energy has the potential to increase our feelings of well-being, anxiety reduction, and communication skills. Discord, contention, and resentment are all manifestations of negative energy. It is important to attract positive energy towards yourself, but repelling bad energy is just as important.

In order to do this, you must raise your energy level and surround yourself with positive vibes. It's a lot less difficult than you may have anticipated! Use these daily keys as a starting point, and you'll see a noticeable rise in your level of positive energy very quickly.

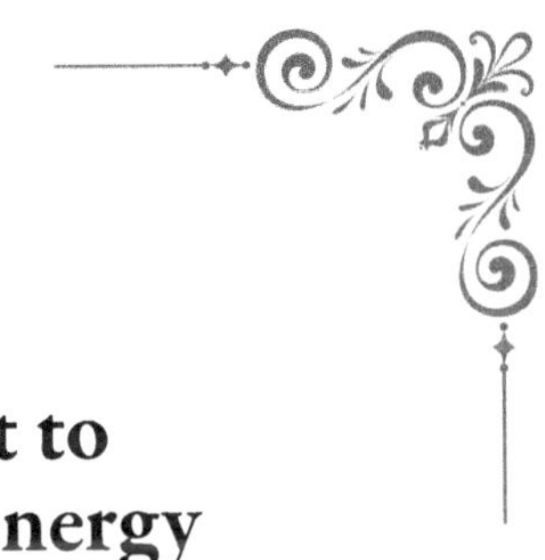

4.1 Take a moment to consider how much energy you're using

When you're continually producing negative energy, it's tough to draw good energy to yourself. Just stop for a minute and consider how others feel when they are in your company. Do you exude a sense of serenity and contentment as a person? Are you a more pessimistic person?

As a consequence of a lack of positive energy, your interpersonal connections will suffer. Regardless of how subtly you do it, the manner in which you approach people will almost always reflect negatively on you. What kind of initial impression do you want to make on folks that come into contact with you and your work?

The fact that others are drawn to you and actively seek you out suggests that you are exuding positive energy. When you're ostracized and neglected, your vibratory state is trapped in a lower, more negative frequency. Concentrate your focus on the positive aspects of life.

4.2 Consider thinking in a new manner

It may be tough to get negative thoughts out of one's head at times. Therefore, it is easy to fall into a condition of pessimism or disinterested thinking. If you wish to attract good fortune, on the other hand, you must listen to your heart rather than your brain. Make an effort to "see the bright side," as the Dalai Lama recommends, and "see the good side." Make an effort to redirect your thoughts the other way when you find yourself thinking negatively.

This may be accomplished by changing the mindset from "I am fighting to adjust to this new environment" to "I am confident that I will be able to overcome these hurdles and adapt to these changes." Resist the temptation to be pessimistic and allow yourself to be caught up in the gloom. Concentrate on the good aspects of your life and don't be concerned about what you don't have. By using the techniques in this book, you can transform your negative thoughts into action-inspiring words that are both positive and founded on reality.

4.3 Take a hard look at your life and get rid of any negative effects that might be there

Negative vibrations may have a negative impact on your feelings of well-being and satisfaction. Positive effects are those that have a negative influence on your life. People, places, and things that have a detrimental effect on your life are instances of negative impacts. In certain situations, you may have people in your life that are harmful to your overall well-being, and you should avoid them. If they are critical or bad, they hurt your self-esteem in some way, and this hurts your self-esteem in some way, too.

Get rid of all of the negative influences in your life and start living the life you want to live. Keep an eye out for negative influences in your life. The only way to completely eliminate their negative influence is to ignore or erase some of them from your life. People who are always in your life should be limited in how much time you spend with them, and you should think about what you want to say before you meet them or talk to them.

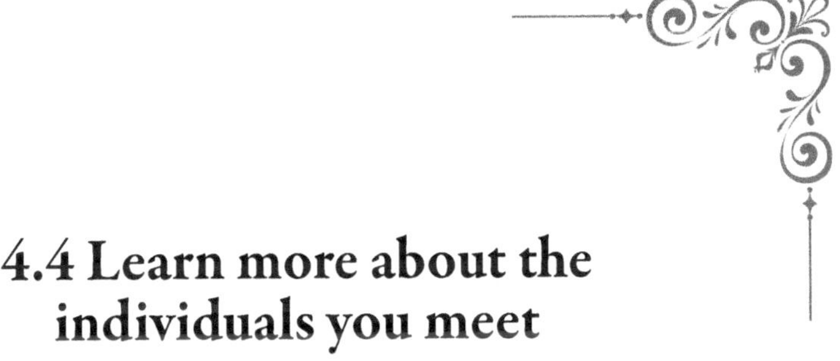

4.4 Learn more about the individuals you meet

In the same manner that you attempt to avoid negative individuals, you should aim to spend time with positive people as well. Join a network of like-minded folks that will serve as an inspiration and motivator for you. If you surround yourself with individuals who bring you pleasure, you'll be happier and more successful in your endeavors.

You may help the group become more energized by bringing your own positive energies to the table. You should look for people who will tell you the truth, but never out of malice or a desire to bring you down, since they are few.

4.5 Don't be afraid to show love and compassion to people who are near you

When people commit little acts of kindness, they benefit both themselves and those who receive them. Individuals who are kind and compassionate to others have been shown to be happier, healthier, and more connected to their family and friends, according to scientific evidence. Giving to others causes you to experience more good feelings, which results in a positive feedback loop.

As a consequence of experiencing kindness and compassion, individuals who have received them are more likely to express kindness and compassion to others. You may show kindness by leaving a lovely message for someone to find, buying the person in line behind you a cup of coffee, or just smiling at strangers. There is a plethora of straightforward approaches to doing this. All of this is a source of joy and positive energy that you may make use of to your benefit.

4.6 Make a habit of being thankful

It's important to set aside some time each day to focus on the many benefits you've had bestowed upon you. If you learn simple techniques for cultivating gratitude, you will be able to replace negative thoughts with positive ones. Every morning, spend a few moments thinking about five things for which you are grateful, and write them down. Once you have finished your exercise, consider one individual for whom you are grateful.

You may wish to keep a gratitude journal to help you stay focused on the good parts of your life and the little joys that bring you joy to help you stay cheerful. List all of the things that have gone wrong in your life and make a note of them. You will be more appreciative of your current situation once you know just how far you've come and how many storms you've weathered along the way.

Chapter 5: The Power of Positive Thought - Your Secret Weapon for Success

To put it another way, thinking positively is the complete polar opposite of negative thinking. According to research, positive thinking happens when you are joyful or when you have accomplished a goal for which you have been striving for a long time, according to research. Paying attention to the little voice in your head may enable you to maintain a more optimistic view of your day throughout the day (the one that is reading these words). Positivity thinking is another method of experiencing good feelings such as joy, excitement, and exhilaration in the present moment. Aside from that, it has the potential to put a grin on our faces and a spring in our step, as well as motivate us to look forward to the future even more. Our brains are always active, whether we are thinking of positive or negative ideas, and some individuals may have a predisposition to think positively more often than others for a variety of reasons, including genetics. Studying positive thinking can be done the same way that learning a language or mastering a subject can be done.

A mind set is the next level up from just thinking happy thoughts from time to time, and it is very possible to attain. You must have a majority of your ideas that are positive in order to have a positive mental attitude. Although common belief holds true in most cases, this is not always the case. The good news is that anybody can teach their minds to reject negative ideas and gloomy attitudes by following tried-and-true methods, utilizing tried-and-true tools, and putting in the necessary time and effort. The point of having an optimistic attitude is not quite clear to me. Having a positive view on life may be advantageous in a variety of situations. Imagine that you're participating in a cross-country or marathon race at a sports day and you're running so hard that your legs are buckling under you and you're experiencing excruciating stifle pain in your thigh. Your energy levels have plummeted, your muscles have deteriorated, and your lungs are on the edge of failing. They'll use positive thinking to get through the difficult periods and win the race, just as so many other great athletes before them have done. Many individuals refer to having a "winner's frame of mind" as a way of describing having a positive attitude about life. After all, who wouldn't want something like that? Positive thinking is also more effective than negative thinking, which is why it is the opposite of negative thinking in terms of how effective it is.

When we make a mistake or fail at anything, we hear voices in our heads telling us that we're stupid. This is referred to as "negative thinking." Individuals who suffer from negative thinking may become mentally ill, preventing them from asking for what they genuinely want in their life to be requested by others as a result of their negative thinking. Others may get concerned about events that may or may not transpire as a result of these circumstances. The ability to have a positive attitude towards life may assist you in making better judgments and doing better in your daily activities. It is lighter and more powerful than the heavier and more debilitating negative energy that is fed by negative ideas, which is fueled by negative thoughts. Inability to maintain a good state of mind and energy is the outcome of having a low amount of both.

Take a look at the following example: In response to an invitation to a party or gathering, many individuals say things like, "I'm not going since no one will like me; I despise those people anyhow." To begin with, do you believe you will be able to meet new people and create a positive first impression on them? It's likely that you won't show up for the event at all. What if you approached the matter with an open mind instead of a closed mentality? "I had a lot of fun changing my appearance! My new shoes are beckoning me to try them on! Getting to know all of these new individuals (and for them to get to know me) is something I'm looking forward to. " At the end of the day, which of these mindsets do you believe will leave you feeling more invigorated, and which one do you believe will actually show up at the party? In order to engage in negative thinking, you must not deceive yourself or pretend to be someone you are not. In your assessments, you must be realistic and honest with yourself. Your brain has the ability to discern whether you are being serious or not. In order to begin thinking positively and living with a positive attitude, we must first learn to notice the wonderful things that occur throughout the day and week.

To be "aware" is to be conscious of one's surroundings. Being conscious means having awareness of your ideas, both happy and unpleasant, and the ability to exercise control over these thoughts is what it means to be conscious. Before you can decide whether anything is beneficial or damaging, you must be aware of what is going on around you and how your own responses to these things affect you. As a consequence, if you want to improve your ability to think positively, you can begin by paying attention to your daily actions. This is necessary in order for you to be able to distinguish between great and negative ideas when they arise in your mind.

Not only can being appreciative of the wonderful things in your life and maintaining a happy attitude aid in your goal-setting, but it will also improve your overall well-being and provide you with joy as well. Additionally, you will be able to see life from a different viewpoint, and your everyday routines will go more smoothly as a result. When you think positively, it spreads like a virus, much like when you smile or laugh! When you're in the company of someone who can't stop laughing because they've just heard a joke or seen something humorous, there's nothing more awkward than being in their presence. Even if they are able to keep their laughter contained for a while, you can't help but join in when they ultimately do so since they are reminiscing about the joke or amusing circumstance in which they were involved. It is likely that your cheerful attitude will have an influence on others in your local vicinity. Keep in mind that for every unpleasant occurrence, there is an equal and opposite happy one.

At any time when you are having a nasty thought, try to think of something positive about it. If you are feeling sad about your employment situation, keep in mind how many people have lost their jobs in the previous few years and are still looking for new ones if you are feeling down about your job situation. As a result of the power of gratitude and positive thinking, you're grateful that you at least HAVE a job, no matter how terrible it is. While sorting through my possessions to get rid of the excess clutter one day, I thought to myself, "This apartment is simply too tiny." I continued with my housekeeping responsibilities (negative thought). After hearing stories about people being forced from their homes due to foreclosure or having their apartments seized because they have lost their jobs, I think to myself, "We are so fortunate and I am grateful that my husband and I are both working so that we can make our payments, have a roof over our heads, and have a place to sleep" (positive thought and gratitude). Having a positive outlook on life is not enough; you must also prepare for success in all you do and take the necessary steps to make that success a reality.

5.1 The Importance of Having a Positive Attitude

Emotions are directly influenced by the ideas that you have in your head at the time. Your emotional well-being is influenced by your thoughts and feelings. Emotions have a role in determining whether or not you are satisfied or unhappy. In the end, whether or not you feel good about yourself, other people, and the rest of the world is totally based on your point of view on these issues. The individuals with whom you spend most of your time in thought have the greatest influence on your life. Your life's most significant events or items are those ones you spend the most time thinking about. Due to the fact that they trigger negative feelings in you (such as wrath and animosity), these people and events are seen as bad by society. They are termed "positive" if they make you feel joyful, balanced, and pleasant in some way.

You have the ability to exert control over your thoughts. In order to gain control over your ideas and beliefs, you must first demonstrate your authority over those thoughts and beliefs. If you want to achieve success, think positively about yourself and be ready to see the best in yourself. There is a clear relationship between positive thoughts and positive conceptions... Bad thinking occurs as a consequence of a person's ideas being unstable and negatively disposed to. When it comes to changing your beliefs and perceptions, conscious effort paired with a strong desire to achieve may make significant strides in your direction. It is possible to increase your general well-being and happiness by making a deliberate decision to think more positively and to open yourself up to new possibilities. Anger, fear, hatred, and envy are all instances of unpleasant feelings that might be experienced by the person who has an idea. Depression and anxiety are caused by unpleasant feelings and/or negative thoughts that keep coming back.

As a consequence, your energy will be depleted, and having a happy and fulfilled existence is necessary for living a fulfilling life. Although it is not always possible, it is possible to think positively while avoiding negative emotions such as anger, fear, or concern. Positive thoughts, according to the definition, are any ideas or notions that make you feel good about yourself, others, or the world in which you are living. All of the recommendations in this area are intended to help you achieve more harmony and peace in your life. If you wish to make changes in your ideas, emotions, and mental habits, you must first become aware of your own thoughts, sentiments, and emotions. As a consequence, the word "mindfulness" has been coined to describe it. The cultivation of self-awareness and self-observation are fundamental components of mindfulness practice. By concentrating on the present moment, you may utilize your purpose and will to transform your thoughts and self-talk from a place of negativity to a place of positivity. Positive ideas need both open beliefs and an open attitude of mind. Both are required for positive thinking. In order to do this, you need to get rid of rigid and constrictive beliefs and replace them with more positive and wide-open ideas.

To save mental energy, you may instead direct it toward your own activities and observations rather than evaluating and analyzing others' actions and observations. It is necessary to forgive oneself and others in order to maintain positive thinking. It is also necessary to let go of one's own and others' wrongdoings, as well as the emotional and psychological hold that previous traumas and injuries have on one. In order to practice positive thinking, one must have a good attitude toward themselves and the environment around them. It may be tough to accept this, particularly if your life experiences and the authoritative people in your life have taught you differently, but it is necessary. However, it is a possibility. In the same way that there are several ways to perceive yourself and others, there are numerous ways to see the world. Rather than seeing failure and injury as setbacks, you should view them as teaching opportunities to improve your performance. Then let them go from your presence, and you will be liberated. The development of a positive mindset is dependent on this. In certain cases, rigid beliefs might lead to negative thinking. In particular, dogmatic attitudes and beliefs about oneself and others are very harmful because they lead to the formation of opinions and the application of judgmental thinking. This is especially true when it comes to the persistence of dogmatic attitudes and beliefs. A person's unpleasant feelings are made worse by their opinions and judgments because they make them feel better about themselves and more superior to other people.

Because of this, a series of furious and sometimes cruel thoughts begin to develop. Indulging in feelings of rage and making harsh statements and behaviors may have a variety of unforeseen consequences when these sorts of emotions are indulged in. Expanding your thinking capacity, letting go of negative or inflexible viewpoints, and halting the incessant flow of opinion and judgment thoughts are all essential for developing outstanding ideas and positive thinking patterns. Concentrate on honing your critical-thinking abilities and deferring the expression of your own thoughts to the greatest degree feasible. Allow yourself to be carried along by the water. The idea is to prevent a full-fledged battle of wills. As a result, there is a steady stream of negative ideas and mental processes running through one's head. Accept people for who they are and what they believe in, without judging them or condemning them. Please do not attempt to change them in any way.

When you attempt to exert influence on others, you will almost certainly find yourself in difficulties. Only you have the ability to effect change. Concentrate all of your efforts on completing the work at hand. Conscious thoughts are impacted by subconscious ideas, which in turn influence conscious thoughts. When you replace your "negative and rigid" beliefs with "positive and open/flexible" beliefs, positive thinking and positive thought patterns become possible for you to pursue. Also essential is accepting good and loving thoughts about yourself, as well as purging your conscious and subconscious memories of the past and prior injuries. Aside from that, as a result of this shift in viewpoint, the negative and critical inner voices will be replaced with a loving and positive one. Positive affirmations, as well as meditation and visualization techniques, may help you change your beliefs and broaden your perspective. The techniques described below can help you do this. In order to think positively, you must first allow yourself to be filled with genuine love by opening your heart to others. Because of this, you will be filled with continual calm and happiness in the interior of your body. You may find it harder to recall pleasant experiences when you are feeling unhappy.

It is thus necessary to have a lasting feeling of serenity and happiness that lasts throughout one's life. In addition to using the meditation and visualization techniques outlined below, you may do this by letting go of any unpleasant feelings you've been holding onto, such as anger, fear, worry, sadness, and guilt, and letting go of those emotions. Positive thinking entails letting go of grudges, forgiving people, and letting go of the past, among other things. These are the thoughts that cause you to be offended, angry, terrified, or saddened by someone else's behavior or words, and they are fueled by your own beliefs. Consider shifting your point of view in order to prevent being upset. Allow yourself to put your ideas on hold and just focus on the present moment. If you practice mindfulness, you may be able to put an end to unpleasant thoughts and feelings. If you live your life through your senses rather than your ideas, you will be happier, more balanced, and more serene. Putting your attention on something useful and beneficial may take various forms, including work, errands, school, or just having a good time. In terms of the process, these are thoughts that are captivated by the specifics of what is going on. This means that, rather than concentrating on the past or looking forward, they are concepts that are grounded in the present moment. In your thoughts, you're flooded with happy recollections of loved ones, friends, pets, and other cherished belongings. Having bad thoughts that are based on your horrific history, terrifying present, or the individuals who have harmed you is not uncommon.

As a result of these negative thoughts and sensations drowning out the positive ones, there is an accumulation of negative energy in the body. Due to the creation of even more sad conceptions and thoughts as a result of this negative energy, it is detrimental. The term "positive thinking" refers to thoughts that are focused on a certain goal. Lots of negative thinking is characterized by being disorganized and erroneous, to name a few descriptive adjectives. Negative thoughts are more likely to originate on the side or at the rear of the brain than on the front. Positive ideas are more likely to originate in the middle of the forehead, which is the most powerful location for them to do so. Unless we take control of our thoughts, they will become disorganized and unpleasant to think about. The development of a negative inner voice is often the result of an inability to concentrate one's thoughts. When one hears this negative inner voice, it is common for them to pass judgment on themselves and others. Concepts that are oriented around details and processes are excellent concepts that are concentrated in their application. These individuals are not preoccupied with thoughts about the future or other issues. As opposed to focusing on the future, they are more concerned with the present—their employment, their hobbies, errands, family gatherings, and vacations, among other things. There is no consideration given to "what if" situations or future possibilities in these reflections. The only thing motivating them is a lack of a desire for vengeance or retribution. Thoughts that are concentrated, focused, and well-balanced are ones that will be beneficial in the long term.

They're the kinds of thoughts that help you stay focused on the work at hand. It is understandable that they would be preoccupied with the specifics of their approach. Despite the fact that the primary emphasis would be on establishing and executing plans, this is the stage at which the emphasis would be on the particular and fine aspects of the plan that was being designed. Creating and implementing plans for work, errands, pleasure, and time off are examples of positive thinking principles. Negative thoughts are those that are centered on one's own ego or self-importance. The concept of egotism refers to a belief that makes you uncomfortable with yourself and with your existing situation. Negative self-or other-judgment thoughts include concepts that make you feel like a victim, ideas that make you feel self-pity, ideas that make you feel fear, and ideas that make you feel rage or hatred. As a consequence of these ideas, other people may be deceived, injured, or misled, which is dangerous. A good attitude toward oneself is one that places the soul above one's ego when it comes to decision-making. It is possible to reach this goal through the use of meditation and visualization techniques.

This approach, in addition to relaxing the ego, inhibits negative ideas, harmful thinking patterns, and a critical inner voice through the use of visualization. Using your willpower, you may regain control of your ideas and cultivate a more positive inner voice for yourself. You'll have to apply mental discipline in order to do this. The core of your intention is located in the centre of the top of your skull. Your attention is drawn to the centre of your forehead, just where your brows come together. With your eyes closed, you have the most power over your thoughts from the center of your forehead. Concentrate on the good aspects of your life and let go of your inner critic. As a consequence, techniques such as meditation and visualization are necessary. There may be occasions when you experience bad thoughts and feelings. If at all possible, use positive thinking to decrease their influence and learn how to cope with them when they do occur. Attempting to suppress unpleasant thoughts and sensations is a bad idea. It is important to recognize when they occur and to be grateful for what they might teach you about yourself and others. It's common for them to share their opinions about people and things that bother you, as well as how to cope with particular circumstances in order to retain a positive attitude towards life. It is not uncommon for the worst to serve as a springboard for greater things to come. When dealing with a difficult issue, it is feasible to start with the negative and work your way up to developing strategies for coping with it and attaining success. As has already been said, the things and people you concentrate on become the most significant things and people in your life as time progresses.

As a consequence, instead of concentrating on negative individuals, pictures, and objects, it is more beneficial to concentrate on positive ones. Your emotions are impacted by the ideas that you have. With practice, you will be able to direct and concentrate your thoughts in order to attain a happy and comfortable emotional state of consciousness. In order to pull it off, you'll need to have the necessary willpower and resources to get things done. Instead of thinking about something terrible, try thinking about something else instead of that awful thing. Your brain is only capable of concentrating on one thing at a time. Using the strategies of substitution and distraction, you may learn to cope with unpleasant ideas. Substitute: Positive ideas and pictures should be used to replace negative ones.

Instead of worrying about what you're thinking about, think about or visualize individuals in your life who are pleasant, kind, and worthy of your time and attention. Consider visualizing yourself with your favorite pet or in a situation that makes you feel joyful and elevated as an alternative to thinking about your problems. Completely inhale and exhale, or count your breaths and concentrate on the number of breaths you take in and out. If you continue in this manner, the negative thoughts will soon go away. The ability to redirect your attention to the present moment allows you to take your mind off of what you are doing and what you are dealing with, which is a positive development.

All of your thoughts, feelings, and actions should be concentrated entirely on the present moment. Don't even think about it for a second. Whatever occurs, it doesn't worry you in the least. Both the past and the future are unimportant at this point. Concentrate on the present moment. It is vital that you pay attention to all areas of the project: the approach, the content, and the details.

Take care not to allow your thoughts to take you away from the present moment, no matter where they may be taking you on their journey. Stop what you're doing and take a deep breath every now and then because this will happen. Take care not to allow your worries to dominate the pleasant times that come along in your life. Fighting negative thoughts with a smile, shutting your eyes, and deep breathing are all helpful methods of coping with them. For a few deep breaths in and out of your chest or belly, your attention is only on your breathing. You may also choose to just stop thinking. By putting your hand over your heart, you may direct your energy there. It's time to just be in the present moment. Focus on your body and senses instead of your thoughts in order to fully immerse yourself in the present moment and stay in the now.

Consider yourself a bystander. You should allow yourself to let go of any preconceived notions about your current state of mind. It's always there for you when you need it. To divert one's attention away from bad thoughts, one might listen to music, pray, or recite mantras. Pay close attention to the songs and prayers, especially the words and melodies. By concentrating on music, prayer, and mantras, you can keep your mind from wandering to negative thoughts. People you encounter should be the center of your attention. Hence, engage with them in a good manner by using positive words and actions. Instead of thinking about or seeing someone who has injured you or whom you despise, think about or see pictures of nice people and animals that you like and that offer you pleasure instead of someone who has hurt you or whom you dislike.

5.2 What Are the Advantages of Maintaining a Positive Attitude?

Although optimism is a powerful weapon, it is worthless if it is not followed up by action. In comparison to just thinking about something for a short period of time, it is more like a way of life. You may use this strategy to produce positive affirmations that can be used to neutralize negative ideas and doubts while also boosting your self-confidence. This approach can be used to battle negative thoughts and doubts while also boosting your self-esteem. It is true that positive thinking is a learned talent that can be honed through repetition, but is it really worth the effort and time it takes to master? Pollyannaish is a phrase used to describe someone who has a naive and excessively optimistic outlook on life, who overlooks the unpleasant aspects of life and only focuses on the positive aspects of life. So, what are your thoughts?

What are your feelings about the situation? In your mind's eye, how do you feel about them? We all have a propensity to concentrate on the bad aspects of our lives, yet finding a positive viewpoint is almost as simple as finding a negative one in the majority of situations. When we engage the law of attraction by focusing on the good and drawing better conditions into our lives, we have the potential to have an influence on our subconscious mind. Never forget that you should keep your focus on the positive and hope for the best, but did you know that thinking about the bad may be as exhausting as thinking about the good? Positive attitudes among employees may be impacted by a company-wide culture of optimism that pervades all levels of the organization. Individuals have been reported to have achieved a successful or unsuccessful outcome solely dependent on their state of mind before beginning the work. It is not enough to just believe in the power of positive thinking.

To be successful in life, you must put your positive thinking skills to work and make them your default view of life's circumstances. By concentrating on the present moment, you may be able to boost your feeling of security and get closer to your objective. First and foremost, in order to become a positive thinker, one must understand the distinction between positive and negative thinking. The term "positive thinking" is often misunderstood by the general public, leading some to believe that money will fall from the sky or that God will ride into town and take away all of our woes, among other things. Despite the fact that this would be perfect, it is unlikely to come to pass. However, by maintaining a positive attitude and being open to new ideas, you will be less inclined to give up and give up. To be optimistic, you must first have a positive attitude towards life. It comes down to the same question as in the chicken-and-the-egg conundrum: which came first, the chicken or the egg?

If you have a pessimistic view on life, you will never consider altering your way of thinking. On the other hand, if you have a positive outlook on life, you will consider changing your attitude. What you say in response to this age-old question on positive thinking and attitude might indicate a great deal about your view on life, your relationship with yourself, and whether or not you are an optimist. Positive thinking and a cheerful demeanor may do wonders for a person's overall health and well-being.

Chapter 6: Ways to Boost Your Mental Well-Being

"Mental health" refers to the state of your whole mental well-being. The quality of your relationships, the strength of your self-esteem, and your ability to regulate your emotions and deal with hurdles are all factors in this assessment.

Everyone has the potential to have problems with their mental or emotional well-being at some point in their life, and for many of us, this will be the case for the rest of our lives. One in every five Canadians suffers from mental illness or drug addiction.

- These suggestions may help you feel better, be more resilient, and have a better experience in life in general.
- Make social engagement, especially one-on-one interactions, a top priority.
- No matter how valuable phone conversations and social media platforms are, there are few things that can match genuine face-to-face interaction with individuals.
- Participating in regular activities might help you maintain a healthy lifestyle.

Physical activity is beneficial to the mind in the same way that it is to the body. One of the several advantages of regular physical exercise is stress reduction. Other advantages include cognitive improvement and enhanced sleep.

- Inquire about something with a second or third individual.
- Make direct eye contact with a friendly individual. Engaging in a face-

to-face discussion with someone you care about is one of the most effective stress-reduction tactics available to us today.

- Make use of your five senses to aid in your understanding.

In fact, when I listen to lively music, I don't find it very relaxing. Do stress balls have the ability to assist you in regaining your center of gravity? What do you think of taking a walk in the woods and taking in the sights and sounds of the natural world? Experiment with several sorts of sensory input to see which ones work best for you.

- Make it a point to relax on a regular basis.
- Yoga, mindfulness, meditation, and other ways to relax may help you feel less stressed.
- Downtime and silent thought should be given top priority.

Regular downtime is essential for one's mental and emotional well-being. As you go about your day, take a moment to relax, think, and take note of the positive aspects, no matter how small they may seem to you. Because they're so easy to forget, make a mental note of them if necessary. Then, when you're feeling down, you may think of them and get a boost.

In order to keep your mind in a good mood, eat foods that are good for your brain.

Omega-3-rich fatty fish (such as salmon), nuts (walnuts, almonds, cashews, and peanuts), legumes (such as kidney beans), green leafy vegetables (such as spinach, kale, and Brussels sprouts), and fresh fruits such as blueberries are all excellent sources of mood-enhancing nutrients.

- At any cost, avoid skipping sleep.
- As you can see, this has a higher influence than you may expect. A good night's sleep may be achieved by avoiding screens for at least two hours before retiring for the evening hours.
- Find a reason for your existence and stick to it
- Every individual's experience with this will be different. There are many options here that are worth pursuing:
- Make a contribution that makes you feel significant and deserving of

recognition.

- People who are important to you deserve your time and attention, so be kind to them.
- As a volunteer, you have the opportunity to broaden your horizons and become a better person.
- Taking care of others may be both rewarding and difficult at times.

Chapter 7: Motivating Yourself in Unexpected Ways

"Most people attempt to improve at least one element of their lives at any given time." To begin with, though, it may be tough to get the guts to take the plunge. It's important to know what motivates you so that you can come up with your own ways to boost your energy levels.

7.1 What is the source of a person's motivation?

- To be motivated is to have a strong desire to achieve one's goals or to meet one's requirements in order to succeed. As a consequence of these developments,
- How ardently are you committed to reaching your goal?
- Something to take with you when you go
- Personal ambitions and aspirations
- What are some of the advantages of having a strong sense of mission?
- It is critical to keep oneself motivated for the following reasons:
- This ensures that you have a target to shoot for.
- It helps you discover answers to your issues and find solutions.
- It makes it simpler to stop engaging in harmful actions.
- It is a tool for overcoming hurdles and embracing new opportunities.
- Increasing one's desire to succeed

The presence of mental health conditions such as depression and anxiety might make it even more difficult to feel motivated. Here are a few pointers:

- Make a single, clearly stated, and realistic goal for yourself to work toward.
- Put a deadline on it and figure out how you're going to achieve your goal, and you'll be well on your way to success (such as in a week).
- Break your goal down into small portions and set up recurring reminders to keep you on track to achieve your objective.
- Keep in mind that you should discuss your goals with your family and friends, and encourage them to assist you in sticking to your plan.

- Methods for staying on top of things
- Make a habit of reminding yourself of your goal on a regular basis by keeping a notebook or downloading an app.
- The use of positive self-talk may be quite useful in the treatment of depression and anxiety. Saying "I'm sorry, but I can't" is a cop-out. "I'll give it a shot" is a more effective response.
- Meditation, mindfulness practice, and other techniques make it much simpler to relax and concentrate.
- Participate in a support group or enroll in a course. Support groups may be equally as beneficial as professional assistance in certain cases.
- When you reach a goal or complete a step, give yourself a reward.

7.2 Efforts to maintain one's motivation

Here are a few pointers:

- Regularly examine your aims and progress to ensure that you are on the right track for your future. Seeing improvement drives you while also increasing your self-esteem at the same time.
- Create new goals on a regular basis and work toward achieving them. Is there anything specific you plan to achieve in the next several weeks? When do you think the next month will be? What will happen in the next year? Concentrate on a single goal at a time in order to prevent being overburdened.
- Don't take your foot off the gas. Maintaining the momentum and consistency of a new habit may help the habit become more automatic over time.
- A mentor is someone who has knowledge and experience in the area in which you would want to see a change in your behavior, such as a teacher or a counselor. Joining social or support groups that include members with similar interests might help you find mentors.
- Make sure you're surrounded by people who will motivate and encourage you. Having supportive friends and family members may assist in lessening the feelings of melancholy and anxiety by encouraging you to use more positive language in your thoughts.
- Exercise may help you maintain or improve your mental health if you include it in your daily routine.
- What to do in the case of a dearth of creative inspiration
- Even if you have a setback, developing resilience will enable you to

keep going and resume where you left off before. Here are a few tips to assist you in regaining your motivation:

- By doing a feasibility study, you can verify that your goals can be accomplished within the time frame you've set for yourself. Perhaps your goal should be split down into smaller, more doable chunks of time.
- It is important not to forget why you set out to achieve the goal in the first place.
- Speaking with a mentor or family member who has achieved similar goals as you may offer you the motivation to continue on your path toward success.
- Sometimes all you need is a fresh start and a break from your routine.

Chapter 8: Role of Self-Confidence

If you don't believe in yourself, you'll only be able to have a limited number of life experiences. Because of your poor self-esteem or lack of self-confidence, you are unable to take advantage of this little gain. A strong feeling of self-worth will give you greater self-assurance and faith in your interpersonal abilities as a result of these traits. This result will be influenced by a number of different circumstances. At this point in your work life, you have a strong feeling of self-worth and pride in your accomplishments. Messages you get from individuals around you, both directly and indirectly, influence your perception of the world and how it works. As children age and become adults, I am certain that if parents were more conscious of the critical role, they play in forming their children's self-esteem and maturity, I am confident that they would pay more attention to what their parents say and do to them.

Parental ways of reprimanding mistakes and imparting essential lessons, as well as a lack of agreement on fundamental matters, have a profound impact on children's self-perceptions. How their adult children react to deceit and life's obstacles is directly influenced by their own adolescent self-confidence, which is discussed in more depth further down in this section. When a person reaches the age of majority, the implications of growing up in a non-nursing environment become obvious.

This characteristic may be shown by someone who is always concerned about the interests of others rather than oneself. In addition, the fact that they are exploited rather than experiencing the good sensations that come from assisting another person contributes to their low self-esteem. People will be pressured to accept and approve of it, regardless of how they feel about it at the moment. It is entirely up to you whether or not you need help with your self-esteem. The most potent kind of encouragement is to attract people into your life who will totally support you and only provide you with the best of what they have to give. Therefore, negative feelings such as poor self-esteem and uncertainty will be less prominent. When you see a successful person in action, it is probable that you will note that they exude a strong sense of self-assurance. Before embarking on a new adventure, many people, even those who have made a lot of money, have their own doubts about their own abilities that they have to deal with.

Exercising one's driving skills on the open road teaches that accomplishment and self-confidence are inextricably linked and mutually reinforcing elements. Being self-assured has a variety of advantages, both in your personal life and in your professional life, including in your company and in the advancement of your career. It is necessary for you to learn to put your trust in other people in order to achieve your life objectives and dreams. You must also learn to overcome any doubts or lack of confidence that you may experience along the path. Having a positive attitude towards life helps in the establishment of a solid basis for trust between people. People who think about bad things all the time will have a hard time meeting their current and future goals.

As a consequence, positive thinking will assist you in growing, helping you to overcome difficult circumstances and speeding up your growth when you feel like you can't go on anymore. Even though there is a positive relationship between success and self-confidence, this is not a certain conclusion. Self-confidence is often incorrect, especially among those who are selfish. It is possible for them to demonstrate a high degree of trust in the face of scrutiny, which is essentially a mixture of vanity and self-delusion combined with naiveté. However, just because someone is confident doesn't mean that they will be good at what they do.

If someone has poor self-esteem, they may be able to pull off an incredible achievement if they have enough confidence. Some individuals are unable to revel in the glory of their accomplishments due to a lack of confidence and a feeling of value in their own abilities. The opposite is true: in most situations, trust and riches may be seen coexisting in an increasingly harmonious condition.

All of your efforts should be focused on slowly building trust, knowing full well that only by doing so will you be able to effectively navigate the positive transition that is occurring over time. Whatever your social awkwardness or confidence level, you can achieve success in whatever area of life you choose to focus on. If you keep your objectives and inhibitions in mind, as well as being prepared to put in the necessary effort to achieve your goals and overcome your lack of self-confidence concerns, you will be successful in the long run. Even if you are intrinsically optimistic, you must establish a solid relationship between your degree of self-confidence and your path to professional achievement in order to be successful. In the absence of coordination and harmony, excessive confidence may ultimately undermine your achievements, whilst a lack of confidence may result in a fall just as you reach the pinnacle of the corporate ladder.

Chapter 9: Finding the Positive in Every Situation

Half-empty glasses are often mistaken for half-full glasses, despite the fact that they are really half-full. When imagining a scenario, people prefer to focus on the negative aspects of the circumstance rather than the positive aspects. Taking the time to reflect on the numerous blessings in our lives, starting with the wonder of being born as a human being, we will discover that we have a lot to be grateful for, if we only take the time to consider them. Even in the most difficult of situations, we can always find a cause to express our gratitude to the creator of the world. This is true even in the most difficult of circumstances. There is always a silver lining to every situation. When we are thankful, we reduce the amount of time we spend feeling scared or frightened, or sad or unsatisfied, and instead we spend that time being grateful. This is a positive frame of mind. As a result, rather than wasting this priceless opportunity, we should make the most of it by remaining committed to our spiritual purpose. It is true that the more time we spend worrying about our circumstances, the less time we have to achieve our objectives. It is possible for two people to attend the same event together. People may spend a significant amount of time blaming others, moaning about the meal, and feeling disappointed as a result of their expectations not being realized. It is possible for the other person to take pleasure in mixing with the other guests and picking items from the buffet that appeal to his or her palate.

They're both in the same spot at the moment. The other individual, on the other hand, is more concerned with identifying the good and enjoyable things in life. When asked about their party experience, one would claim they had a horrible time, while the other would say they had a wonderful time. Which of the two will feel the most elated and energized after the event is the most important question. In a similar vein, we are continuously confronted with a diverse spectrum of scenarios and circumstances. One may choose to concentrate on the negative and complain or be dissatisfied for the rest of one's life, or one can choose to focus on the positive and enjoy and be pleased with what one has. Keeping our attention on the positive and engaging in spiritual thoughts and activities may aid us in our spiritual development. When we have negative ideas bouncing around in our heads, we might be wasting important time that could be spent focusing on God's presence. Always look for the positive aspects of every circumstance. In the face of hardship, we have the option of choosing to see the positive side of things and making the most of our limited human existence.

9.1 Perceiving the good in others may assist you in being happy in your own life

In accordance with research, folks who surround themselves with optimism have a greater proclivity to recognize the good in others. The same is true when looking at it from the opposite direction. The practice of looking for the good in others has been shown to increase one's level of optimism and happiness in those who do it often. Understanding the good in others necessitates us confronting our own prejudices, but the effort is well worth it. We've had decades to build our impressions of people and their actions by the time we're in our 50s and 60s. Some of them may be realistic, depending on our own personal prejudices, while others may not. Because of these and other factors, we must constantly remind ourselves to look for the good in others if we are to really appreciate our golden years. The fact is that no matter how close we get to someone, they will remain a mystery to us. We are all creatures of our own brains, and it may be difficult to discern what other people's intentions could be at times. When we are conscious of who we are, it is much easier to come up with rationalizations for our own behavior. We, on the other hand, are considerably less tolerant of others' mistakes. Our self-forgiveness becomes stronger when we arrive at work earlier than expected. We are ready to characterize someone who drives recklessly as a jerk as a result of his actions and words. During this process of brainstorming wonderful alternatives to other people's negative behaviors, your anger will lessen and your optimism will soar. On the other hand, it is simple to make judgments about someone based on a small quantity of information. When we hear someone shout, the phrase "angry person" immediately comes to mind. In the event that a friend declines our invitation or expresses disagreement with our point of view, it is simple to conclude that they do not like us. To add insult to injury, once we have formed an opinion about someone, it is quite difficult to alter our minds and view them in a different light in subsequent years. Negative transformation necessitates the difficult but necessary step of refraining from passing judgment. Each one of them has their own past and a distinct narrative to tell. Their resemblances to us are considerably more numerous than we realize. Despite their tremendous value, they are similar to you in that they have defects that distinguish them from the crowd. What other people are thinking continues to be a mystery to us. It is critical to give them the benefit of the doubt since they have earned it.

Almost everything that occurs in our lives is influenced by our encounters with other people. Making friends with someone who is like you in that they are doing the best they can with the circumstances they find themselves in is a pleasant experience. Some of us may choose to alter our conduct in order to compensate for our biases and prejudices at certain points in our lives. Although we may be unable to let go of our anger, we may be able to recognize the triggers that cause us to lose our cool. The awareness of our own triggers may enable us to realize when we are passing harsh judgment on others or ourselves. When we learn to recognize anger, there is a chance that we may learn to replace it with laughter as a result of the process of recognizing it. When we consider the absurdity of human existence, we may find ourselves amused. It takes more than just avoiding bad feelings to achieve true self-acceptance; one must also be able to grasp oneself in order to do this. As long as you believe in your own goodness, you will be able to approach people with an open heart and an open mind.

What is it about yourself that you admire the most? Is this something you're on the lookout for in other people as well? Perhaps, in order to perceive goodness, we must embrace human nature as it is, with all of its flaws and defects. Everyone has something to teach us if we are willing to listen and take the time to learn. Even the most negative individuals may assist us in gaining a more accurate understanding of our own limitations and abilities. In an interview, Elisabeth Kubler Ross once said to me, "We frequently despise the characteristics in other people that we despise the most in ourselves." She was absolutely correct in everything she stated. This is something that I am absolutely dedicated to believing. It's conceivable that our sentiments of animosity are being exaggerated by our own minds. Whether we recognize ourselves in their actions and words, or whether we see ourselves reflected in them, is a matter of perspective. Sometimes you'll come across someone who will have a long-term detrimental influence on your health. This isn't uncommon. When this occurs, cut them off immediately. A person's need to be understood is more often than not disguised under a mask of fury or pride, and it is this desire that you will unearth. Listening is a vital life skill that may be learned quickly. The fact that it is so difficult makes it almost hard to pay attention to what others are saying throughout their presentations.

As a culture, we spend much too much of our time passively waiting for the opportunity to express our views. When we put in the effort to first understand them and then to be understood by them, we can't help but recognize the good in the people around us. As long as you devote your whole focus to the task at hand, you will be showered with admiration and encouragement. We are just as eager to forgive ourselves as we are to criticize others. A vital source of enjoyment and optimism has been cut off from us as a result of this decision. It is impossible not to notice the good in others' actions once we make the effort to understand their thoughts and intentions in their entirety. In addition, when we seek the good in others, we realize that we aren't the only ones on the planet with good intentions. In terms of learning from one another, we have a lot to gain as a group. Because the more we strive to recognize the good in others, the more likely it is that we will see the good in ourselves as well. Embracing our flaws, and I mean this literally, will get us much closer to actual joy than anything else we can do.

9.2 Get in the habit of looking for the positive aspects of every scenario

Every day, whether in our personal or professional lives, we are confronted with a variety of obstacles to contend with. When it comes to our professional lives, there is a continual sense of uncertainty, as well as the possibility of being trapped in a negative feedback cycle. The effort to find work, the strain of competing with your coworkers, the lack of support from family members, and the never-ending bombardment of demands are all factors to consider. You have a remedy for any problem you are experiencing. To put it another way, you should train your brain to look for the positive aspects of everything it comes into contact with. Many individuals these days rely on their jobs to provide a significant portion of their income.

Chapter 10: It's Time to Discover Who You Really Are

Understanding who we are as people is the most essential journey we will ever undertake in our life. Unfortunately, a great percentage of us go about our everyday lives either completely unconscious of what we're doing or listening to our own inner critic, who feeds us all sorts of lies about ourselves. Self-awareness is seen as a kind of self-indulgence, and we go about our lives without ever pondering the most crucial question of all: What is my life's purpose? "Who am I, at the end of the day?" It is an issue of "what you desire to accomplish with your one wild and precious life," in the words of poet Mary Oliver. It may seem to be a self-centered objective, yet it is vital to all we accomplish in life since it is a process of self-sacrificing effort on our part. It is necessary to understand ourselves and our place in the greater scheme of things before we can be the greatest mate or parent. It is equally critical to understand what we can do to help the world and how we might go about doing it. Anyone may enjoy the benefits of going on a personal journey and reaping the benefits of doing so. The process includes removing layers that no longer serve us and don't correctly represent who we are in the real world as part of its breakdown and elimination phase.

But in order to go forward, we must first recognize our own potential and then work tirelessly toward fulfilling our own unique destiny, whatever that may be. This is a massive project on many levels. Being open and sensitive at the same time necessitates us being aware of our own unique strength and potential. In its role as an intriguing new acquaintance, it is not something to be dreaded or avoided at all costs, but rather something to be sought out with the same attention and care that we would show to our own new acquaintances. These considerations have resulted in the creation of the following list of seven of the most beneficial things to engage in while on this incredibly private trip. The first and most important step is getting to know ourselves so that we can understand what makes us tick and why we behave in certain ways. That means we must understand our own particular narrative in order to proceed. Making the decision to be fearless and ready to learn about our history is an important step in the process of understanding ourselves and what we want to become. More than a few studies have indicated that it is not just the events that have happened in our lives that shape who we become, but also how well we have made sense of those occurrences. It is possible for someone's current behavior to be affected by their past behavior, especially if they have been through a lot of traumata.

It has been discovered by experts that there is a "statistically significant relationship" between one's psychological well-being and the coherence of one's life narrative. According to Dr. Daniel Siegel, our capacity to make informed, conscious judgments in the present rests on our ability to construct a "coherent narrative" of our past that correctly depicts our current selves. As adults, our beliefs and upbringing have a significant impact on the way we act and behave. Individuals, according to Dr. Robert Firestone, author of The Self Under Siege, are able to sympathize with their parents' defenses while simultaneously absorbing the critical or antagonistic views that were directed at them while they were young. When a child grows up and is exposed to harmful personal attacks, he or she develops a foreign system known as the anti-self, which interferes with and opposes the formation of a true identity. " As adults, we have a tendency to identify and defend ourselves based on our childhood experiences. Almost always, they make us feel uncomfortable and have an unintentional influence on our behavior.

It is possible that having a strict mother as a youngster contributed to a greater feeling of inadequacy as an adult. Fear of being mocked may cause us to grow up defensive or unable to attempt new things because we are afraid of being ridiculed. We can easily see how continuing this uncertainty into adulthood may result in a lack of self-awareness and a limitation of the range of options available to us. First and foremost, in order to break free from this pattern of behavior, one must understand what is driving it. Every opportunity should be used to study the root causes of our most self-limiting or self-destructive inclinations when it is possible. Perhaps our feelings of loss and ignorance are a result of our efforts to hide or disguise our history. In certain respects, it may seem that we are unsure about our own identities. Without considering the reasons for our actions, we may behave without giving them much thought. Mindsight: The New Science of Personal Transformation by Dr. Siegel describes how Dr. Siegel lost his composure after a disagreement with his son. Finally, Dr. Siegel understood that his emotional reaction was a result of preconceived notions about his brother that he had as a youngster rather than his current sentiments for his child. The incident taught him "how many layers of meaning our brains have, and how rapidly earlier memories may return to impact our actions," he wrote in his journal following the event.

As a consequence of these relationships, we may find ourselves performing things without even realizing it. As a result of using a method known as mindsight, Dr. Siegel was able to make sense of his experience. Mindsight is defined as "a kind of focused attention that allows us to explore the interior workings of our own ideas." This gave him the opportunity to speak with his son and fix the situation. "That conflict provided me with insights that assisted me in gaining clarity regarding my own childhood memories, which was a great source of consolation once I obtained mindsight," says the author. Some of the most difficult events in our lives may be turned into learning experiences that help us understand more about ourselves and how we connect with others. When we think in this manner, we get valuable insights about our own conduct and are better equipped to deal with the memories that surface as a result of those discoveries. The outcome of this is that we may be more aware of the more harmful consequences of our past and more actively adjust our behavior in order to better represent how we really think and feel, as well as how we want to be in the present.

10.1 Making the First Steps Toward Your Self-Discovery Process

How frequently have you taken the time to think about your long-term objectives and aspirations? You could be looking for a way to reach your ultimate objectives, regardless of whether you've already made the initial step toward self-discovery. The daily grind makes it easy to lose sight of the significance of your own objectives, values, and even the characteristics that distinguish you from other people. Knowing and acknowledging your own personality traits may provide you with valuable insight into your inner self. On a daily basis, it is vital to maintain focus on certain goals. Contrary to this, a life spent repeating the same activities would not likely provide much joy. If you've ever asked yourself, "Who am I, really?" you've come to a watershed moment in your journey through life. It might be good to think about oneself in order to get a better sense of who one is.

Many individuals identify themselves only by their connections with others or the activities that they have always engaged in, without taking into consideration the option of trying something new. Despite the fact that it may seem paradoxical, you will continue to put the needs of others ahead of your own until you have a clear understanding of what matters most to you and who you want to be personally in the future. We are able to enhance and make more meaningful our lives when we follow our interests. If you went into medicine because you wanted to assist people, you may discover that working in medical billing does not allow you to fulfill your goal of serving others to the extent that you would want. Finding the job that you really desire and studying the processes necessary to make a career transition are two instances of how you might live out your passion in the workplace. Another alternative is to look for volunteer opportunities that will allow you to use your abilities as a street medic to good effect.

The value of following your interests does not imply that you should pursue a job or specialize in a certain area of study. Consider how you use your spare time on a daily basis. Do you engage in any physical activities? Is there anything in your life that gives you a sense of fulfillment and exhilaration? Using people's own interests, such as their favorite movies and music, researchers may get a better understanding of who they are. Self-reflection may assist you in developing new strategies to improve your life and make it more fun. Make time for self-reflection. It's possible that you don't have many hobbies or interests that you'd like to share with your partner. You are more than welcome to participate! For those who have not taken care of themselves in a long time, it is possible that they have forgotten what it was like to engage in relaxing activities once upon a time. Where should you start looking when it comes to seeking a solution to this issue? Try something radically different from what you're used to. Right? Without giving something a chance, how can you know whether it is something you would enjoy? For example, you may have always had an interest in painting, but you haven't done anything with it since taking a pottery class in college. Inform yourself about free or low-cost adult education programs that are available at your local library or other community-based organizations. Online tutorials may be a viable alternative to traditional classroom instruction.

The information they present may not be identical, but it is usually sufficient for you to determine whether or not to investigate the issue further in the future. Everyone has a distinct set of abilities, whether they be in the arts, home renovation, gastronomy, or a variety of other fields. As part of the self-discovery process, you may want to spend some time thinking about your own particular skills and how you can put them to use in the future. On a regular basis, your friends and neighbors may come to you for assistance with party planning or gardening tasks. It's never too early to start putting your newly acquired abilities to work for you. Practicing your abilities may result in an increase in your self-confidence as a result of the enhancement of your abilities. On the other hand, a greater feeling of self-worth may spur you on to further explore these and other abilities that you may have overlooked in the past. Learning is most successful when it is seen as a continuous process that lasts a lifetime. Accept the opportunity to get completely absorbed in an area of study that has always piqued your interest. History or science are two fields where online resources, such as books and manuals, may be useful.

Invest some time in researching your hobbies and seeing what free applications and websites are available to assist you with them; chances are you'll discover something that will benefit you in your academic endeavors. No matter if you want to enroll in a course or learn from another student, or whether you choose to teach yourself a new skill, continuing your education is always a good choice. Many of us can recall the benefits of writing during our adolescence, such as the ability to more fully explore our ideas and feelings via writing. By returning to your work, you may reconnect with yourself and learn more about who you've become as a result of your experiences (or blogging).

Keep a diary to aid in self-reflection, but it may also be used for more practical purposes, such as organizing paperwork. It is entirely up to you how you choose to use your diary. Alternatively, you may use it to ask and answer questions for yourself, or you can use it to go further into any of the concepts offered here. No, I don't consider myself to be a very gifted writer. That is completely OK. At times, just jotting down whatever comes to mind may be really helpful. If you're more artistically inclined, art journaling may be an excellent way to explore your ideas and ambitions in more depth. It's as simple as that: sit down with a piece of paper and a picture of your perfect future and watch what occurs. You may want to try the "tombstone exercise," which is a psychotherapy practice that has been shown to be effective. This includes making a list of the things that are important to you and what you believe in, as well as what you want to be remembered for after you die, which is a crucial part of the process.

Chapter 11: Be A Good Version of Yourself

Isn't it true that you have to love yourself? That being the case, you are not alone in your feelings and thoughts. One of the characteristics of self-love is a sense of worth or value in one's own eyes. There is no need for others to tell us that we are good enough, bright enough, or handsome enough; we are self-aware of these qualities. When we attain these objectives, our self-esteem and self-confidence surge.

When we don't value ourselves, we experience an upsurge in negative feelings and self-centered emotions. For example, we may consider the following:

- Inadequacy
- Shame
- Angry
- Thrilled and enthused (to prove ourselves to others)
- Lonely
- Guilty

11.1 Why It's Important to Love Yourself

If you don't love yourself, it's possible that you'll be more critical of yourself. As an example, you may tell yourself things like "I'm worthless," "I'll never be successful at this," or "I'm not bright enough," among other things. Thinking along these lines might lead to feelings of anxiety, sadness, and despair, among other things.

11.2 How to Develop Self-Esteem

Even if it isn't the most straightforward thing to do, we have the potential to increase the number of positive feelings we have about ourselves. Increasing one's self-esteem may be accomplished via a number of scientifically proven techniques. Keep in mind, though, that they may seem difficult to master at first. It's conceivable that you're not in the mood to treat yourself with the kindness and respect that you deserve at the moment. It is very OK to begin practicing self-love strategies gradually. Here are a few suggestions to get you started:

- Your everyday actions are the first step toward developing self-acceptance.
- Take a look at the people in your life that you adore and appreciate. When it comes to dealing with them, what is your strategy?
- If they have strong thoughts and ideals, you should be patient with them, kind to them, and forgiving of their faults.
- Because you really care about them and believe in their abilities, you provide them with the resources they need to succeed in their endeavors.
- Just take a moment to consider how you are treating yourself right now.
- How do you treat yourself? Do you give yourself the same degree of devotion and respect that you would give to a close friend or a potential romantic interest?

11.3 What level of self-care do you practice these days?

Here are some easy methods to provide your body and mind some self-love on a regular basis:

- Understanding the significance of having a good night's sleep
- Consuming a well-balanced diet
- Make a time commitment to reflect on your religious beliefs.
- Physical activity on a regular basis
- Showing thanks to yourself and the people who are important in your life
- Play whenever the mood strikes you.
- Avoiding undesirable habits and being in the company of individuals who have a negative influence on you,
- Meditation and contemplation are two terms used to refer to the same thing.
- How many of these commonplace activities do you think you'll let yourself do? Is it possible to say that you love yourself on a deep level if this isn't the case?
- A positive attitude about yourself is only one part of self-love. It's also a series of actions and habits that you do every day.
- Accept the pain as it comes.
- Nobody is without flaws. In our modern world, it's easy to think that self-love is the same thing as an endless source of happiness and optimism.
- Some individuals sing God's praises every day, no matter how depressed they are or how hopeless their situation seems to be to them.

- We feel that this is the best course of action since pleasant vibes should attract more positive vibes. We hope you agree.
- Your unshakable optimism, on the other hand, is founded on a sham. It is dishonest to ignore the needs of one half of your existence while the other half is still alive.
- Every single one of us has a dark side that is filled with anguish and sadness, just like everyone else. Our spiritual and mental health suffer as a consequence of our failure to acknowledge these facts.
- Recognize and embrace your genuine self as you have always been. Don't cling to the things from your past that you're ashamed of anymore.
- Recognize that you are capable of experiencing feelings of disdain, rage, and jealousy at various points in your life. In addition, when you find yourself in need of some quiet time, learn to cherish it.
- Spread the word about your opinions and emotions with other people.
- On your path of self-discovery, you will come face to-face with some shocking and alarming truths about yourself.
- However, the goal is to work your way through them and grow to respect yourself more as a result of embracing and recognizing who you really are.
- It only makes sense to find the gems in the rough when you have dealt with your own problems and problems.
- On your journey, these are the attributes that will be of great assistance to you. After you've eliminated everything else, you'll be left with your empathy, spirituality, humor, and love.
- To be able to properly share yourself with others, you must first learn to appreciate and love yourself.
- Don't be scared to be yourself in front of the individuals you come into contact with on your travels. Having discovered the joy of loving oneself, it is now time to begin educating others on how they might experience this feeling too.
- Being confident enough to share personal information about oneself is not always easy to come by.

Chapter 12: Positive Affirmations for Self-Love, Motivation & Better Mental Health

Affirmations are personal declarations that may be used to promote positive and constructive thinking in order to counter negative thinking. Affirmations can be used to battle negative thinking in a variety of situations. These self-love affirmations have been compiled to assist anyone who wants to strengthen their relationship with themselves. Affirmations for self-love may take various shapes and forms, and I hope you will find at least a few that resonate with you among the ones in this collection. The usage of these should be on a consistent basis.

You may repeat these to yourself whenever you are having one of those bothersome negative self-thoughts that you find yourself having. Consider writing them down on a piece of paper and posting them someplace where you will see them on a regular basis.

Every day, as part of your regular routine, repeat the affirmations for self-acceptance and love. Examine your self-perception over time to see if you can detect any changes in your perception.

- I remain cool and relaxed in each scenario.
- My muscles have loosened up, and I feel more at ease.
- My anxiety is dissipating.
- I'm in a good mood and feeling at ease.
- I feel at ease in the presence of others.
- For everything that is wonderful in my life, I am grateful and appreciative.

- Every deep breath I take brings me a sense of calm.
- I'm letting go of all the nasty feelings I've been harboring inside of me.
- I am entitled to a happy and fulfilling existence.
- I'm taking long, deliberate breaths to calm myself down.
- Let go of all my anxieties and concerns, please.
- I am entitled to a life of bliss.
- I feel at peace and serene.
- It's important to me that I'm surrounded by things that make me happy.
- I've decided to shift my emphasis from the negative to the positive.
- Despite how I'm feeling, I know this is just a phase.
- My whole being is enveloped in a sense of peace and contentment.
- It's as though the pace of my thinking has slowed.
- My breathing is rooted in my center, and this breathing is calming to my body and mind.
- My ability to solve problems improves when my body and mind relax.
- I'm taking back control of my life.
- I have a low threshold for anxiety.
- I'm letting go of my anxieties and concerns.
- My life is in my hands.
- Attracting good things into my life is easy for me since I'm an upbeat person.
- I'm well-equipped to deal with this issue.
- I've decided to be cool in the face of this crisis because it will pass.
- I always make intelligent selections because I have faith in my instincts.
- My strength comes from my ability to maintain a calm demeanor.
- I choose pleasure now and every day.
- At this present time, I am unharmed.
- Every second that passes, I become stronger.
- I'm gradually allowing myself to have a sense of serenity inside myself.
- Truthfully, I am surrounded by blessings, love, and encouragement.
- What I don't realize is how much strength I have.
- I have faith in life's unfolding course.
- Everything worked out in my favor.

- There is a sense of peace in my body.
- I'm taking a deep breath and letting go of all the tension in my body.
- I feel secure and in command.
- I'm thankful for the many blessings in my life.
- When things go wrong, I can bounce back.
- To be honest, I have faith in my own resiliency.
- I'm fortunate to have the affection and support of my family and friends.
- As I accept myself, I feel at peace in my mind and in my soul.
- Do I have faith in myself right now!

*Did this book help you in some way?
If so, I'd love to hear about it.
Honest reviews help readers find the right book for
their needs.*

CONCLUSION

It's hard to love yourself when you're constantly surrounded by negative energy. That's why we created this book with tips to help you love yourself more! We hope you enjoyed our book on how to love yourself and boost your motivation.

Many people struggle with feelings of low self-esteem, lack of motivation, and lack of confidence, which can have a huge impact on their mental health. We are here to tell you that you are worth loving and that you deserve to be happy in life. By practicing these skills, you will be able to boost your motivation and mental health in the process. This is a great book to start with if you are just learning to love yourself, and it's an excellent opportunity for you to start feeling good about your life!

Love yourself for who you are, and trust me, if you are happy from within, you are the most beautiful person, and your smile is your best asset.
ILEANA D'CRUZ